GIGGLE TRIBE

By Robert Andrew Speirs
Illustrated by Wendy Speirs

Copyright © 2021 Victory Publishing.

All rights reserved. No part of this publication may be reproduced, distributed, or transmitted in any form or by any means, including photocopying, recording, or other electronic or mechanical methods, without the prior written permission of the publisher, except in the case of brief quotations embodied in critical reviews and certain other noncommercial uses permitted by copyright law. For permission requests, write to the publisher, addressed "Attention: Permissions Coordinator," at the address below.

ISBN: 9781733194150 (Hard Cover)

ISBN: 9781733194174 (Paperback)

First printing edition 2021.

Victory Publishing

Casper, Wy

United states

www.victorybookpublishing.com

To Bob Andrew, our daughters Julie Rose Speirs Rabbani and Cara Speirs Houston. Bob, thank you for leaving us with this delightful story that teaches values of unity, patience, and perseverance. Although you are no longer here physically your presence is always with us. Julie and Cara thank you for your support and encouragement.

The Giggle Tribe meet in their clubhouse.

It's Zak's turn to be the leader.

He brought oatmeal cookies and orange juice for everyone.

He said, "My mom told me, Mayor Ebony is coming to our neighborhood."

Mayor Ebony is planning her visit to see the gardens of Greenbriar.

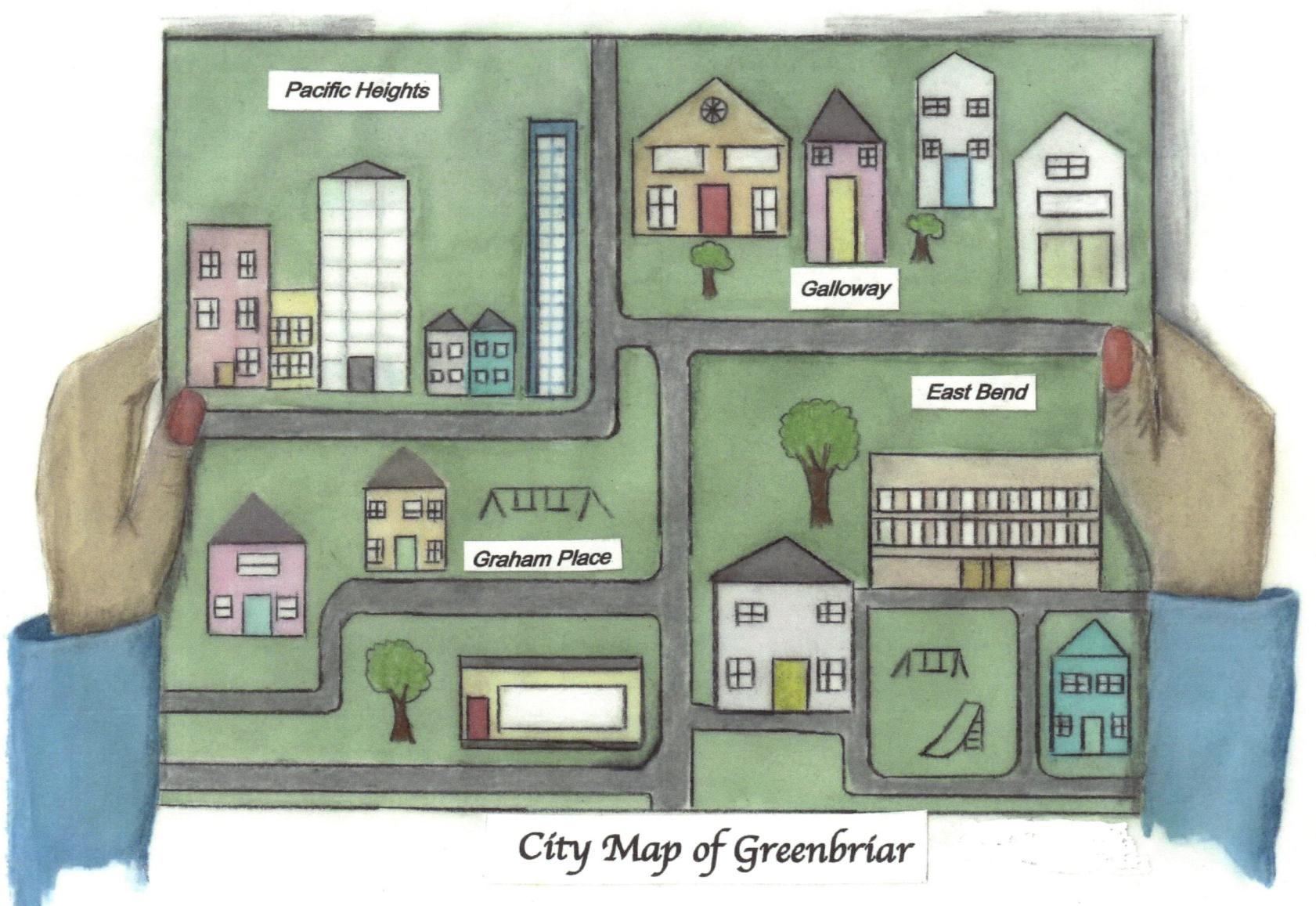

She is looking to find the "Garden of the Year."

The families of Greenbriar are working hard to make their gardens look good for Mayor Ebony.

They carefully plant just the right colors to make their garden special.

Arlo and Emma are helping their parents water their orange, red, and yellow flowers.

She said, "Giggle Tribe, today we need to talk about how we can help the garden problem."

Emma said, "What if all the families share one big garden? Then the Mayor can see how we all work together."

Autumn said, "Giggle Tribe, let's vote. If you agree with Emma's idea put your thumbs up."

Everyone put their thumbs up. Autumn said, "OK Giggle Tribe, looks like we all agree with Emma's idea. We need to tell our parents about the shared garden."

The Giggle tribe voted again, and everyone agreed with Arlo.

The parents liked the idea of the shared garden and spoke with the librarian.

She approved the idea so all of the families brought their flowers to the library and carefully planted them.

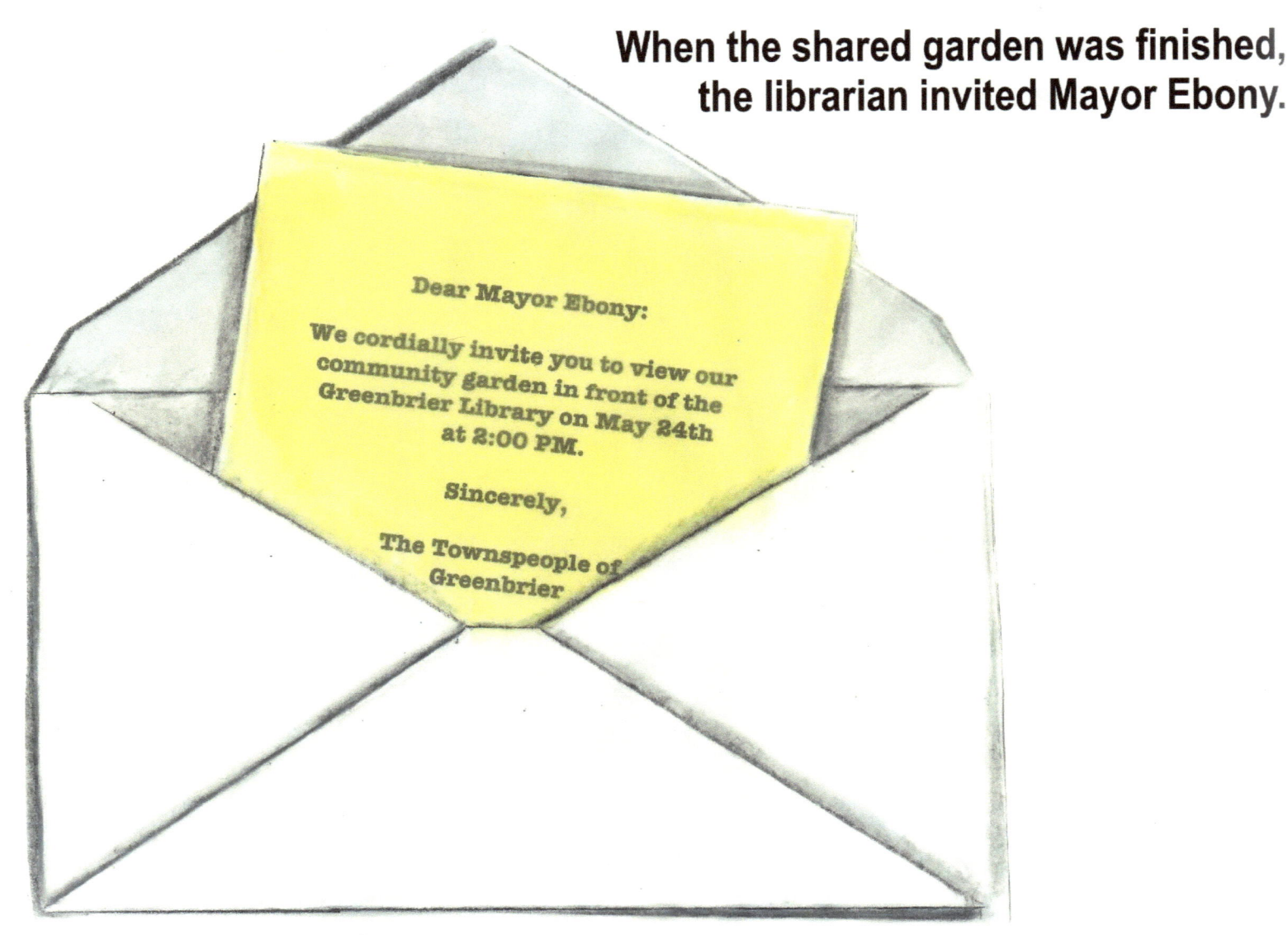

When the shared garden was finished, the librarian invited Mayor Ebony.

All of the families met at the library to welcome Mayor Ebony.

"I would also like to present this Certificate to the Giggle Tribe for their idea of the Shared Garden."

The Giggle Tribe is proud of their certificate and it hangs on the back wall of their clubhouse.

www.ingramcontent.com/pod-product-compliance
Lightning Source LLC
Chambersburg PA
CBHW041819080526

44587CB00004B/142